LAST TA

in Little Grimley

Gordon
Bernard
Joyce
Margaret

Joining The Club

Jenny
Tom

FLYING DUCKS PUBLICATIONS

ISBN 0 9517267 4 9

LAST TANGO
in Little Grimley

The scene is a simple stage, cluttered with remnants of past amateur dramatic productions. There are a number of chairs laid out centre stage, on which sit Bernard, Gordon, and Joyce. As the curtain rises, they are sitting in silence, and looking bored and impatient.

Gordon (*checking his watch*) Well, I suggest we make a start.
Bernard Margaret's not here yet.
Joyce She told me she might not bother this year.
Bernard She always says that. She's just after attention.
Gordon We can't wait all night - it's nearly quarter to.
Joyce She's not going to come now.
Gordon I'm calling the meeting to order. Right, this is the Annual General...

Enter Margaret.

Margaret Sorry I'm late.
Gordon Come on, Margaret, we've already started.
Margaret Is this it?
Gordon I'm afraid so.
Margaret Where's Alan?
Bernard Alan's broken his leg.
Joyce And Jane's got a tupperware party tonight.
Margaret What about Peter and Alice?
Gordon They reckon they're not going to bother this year.
Margaret Oh, they always say that. They're just after attention. I suggest we start without them.
Bernard It's a matter of having to. They're not coming.
Gordon Right, down to the business in hand. This is the Annual General Meeting of Little Grimley Amateur Dramatic Society...
Margaret Point of order.
Gordon (*impatiently*) Yes, Margaret - what is it?
Margaret We should begin by electing our Chairperson for the year.

A Flying Ducks Publication

Gordon Well I was coming to that. It's the first item on my agenda.

Margaret Yes, but deciding the agenda is the job of the Chairperson, whom we have not yet elected.

Gordon It is the job of the incumbent Chairman to decide the best way to vote in the new Chairman.

Margaret Chairperson. It could be a woman.

Gordon All right, Chairperson. Does this really matter?

Margaret Absolutely. What happens if the new Chairperson disagrees with the manner in which the old Chairman decided upon the initial agenda?

Gordon Then the first item on that agenda, namely the voting in of the new Chairperson, is declared invalid, in which case the new Chairperson is no longer the new Chairperson, and controls reverts back to the original Chairman.

Bernard What is this? Yes bloody Minister?

Margaret These things are important, Bernard.

Bernard Look, just cut the crap. Who wants Gordon to be Chairman? (*All except Margaret raise their hands*) And who wants Margaret? (*Margaret indignantly refuses to raise her hand, and merely adopts a haughty look*) Right, that's settled. Let's get on with it.

Gordon Happy now, Margaret?

Margaret Absolutely.

Gordon Right.

Margaret (*under her breath*) I don't envy your job, Gordon.

Gordon Item two - Treasurer's report. Joyce?

Joyce Well, I'm afraid we lost money on our last production.

Bernard That makes a change.

Gordon Don't interrupt, Bernard. Let's have the details, Joyce.

Joyce Well, in total we spent eighty-four pounds and fifty-five new pence.

Margaret Does that include my photocopies?

Joyce That's everything.

Gordon And how much did we take on the door?

Joyce Well, over the three nights, including programme sales, and the revenue from Mrs Marsh's delicious tea-buns, which she kindly donated free of charge - lovely and moist they were - I've got the recipe by the way if anyone...

Gordon Joyce!

Joyce Thirty-seven pounds and four new pence.

Bernard Another blockbuster.

Joyce In retrospect, I think we went a little overboard on the set.

Bernard Overboard? You gave me a budget of twenty-eight quid!

Margaret You didn't have to spend it all.

Bernard Do you realize the cost of conti-board these days?

Gordon All right, all right. It's no good blaming Bernard. It's bigger audiences we need, not smaller sets. Now, some bad news. I received this letter this morning from Stan Fellows.

Margaret Well that's predictable. I suppose the miserable old twat's putting the rent up again.

Gordon Worse than that, I'm afraid. He actually wants us to start paying him some of it.

Bernard Have we not paid him?

Gordon Not for the last three years, no.

Margaret How much do we owe him?

Gordon Four hundred pounds.

Bernard Bloody hell!

Gordon Precisely. And he wants it paid, in full, before the end of the season, or we're out.

Joyce Out?

Gordon Out. Finished.

Margaret Where the hell are we supposed to find four hundred pounds? That's more than we lose in a whole season.

Joyce What about the Arts Council?

Gordon I spoke to the Arts Council this afternoon.

Margaret And?

Gordon They weren't hopeful.

Margaret Meaning what?

Gordon Well, they reckoned that with the amount they'd sponsored our losses over the last three years, they could have re-opened the Old Vic. Apparently they have bets at the office on how much we're going to lose on each production.

Margaret Cheeky sods.

Gordon And I'm afraid we no longer meet their criteria for support.

Margaret What's that supposed to mean?

Bernard I think it means no more money.

Gordon Precisely.

Margaret And what exactly are their "criteria for support"?

Gordon Well, we're not offering theatre for children, or for ethnic or sexual minorities, or prisons, we have no disabled actors, we're just plain...

Bernard Crap.

Margaret Well that's a great attitude. So they no longer support theatre for the masses.

A Flying Ducks Publication

Gordon You can hardly describe our audiences as masses, Margaret. They stay away in droves.

Margaret So, we've had it, then.

Gordon The Arts Council did offer one ray of hope.

Joyce What's that?

Gordon They're not going to ask for their money back.

Bernard Terrific.

Gordon No, I'm afraid there's only one way out of our crisis, and that's to make a huge profit on our next production. (*Cynical laughter from Bernard and Margaret*) Which brings me neatly onto the next item on my agenda - suggestions for the next production. Anybody got any thoughts? Yes, Joyce.

Joyce I'd like us to do (*the others all pre-empt her, and join in*) Seven Brides For Seven Brothers.

Gordon Joyce, I know it's your favourite musical, but I have to say, I can foresee a few...logistical problems with us doing Seven Brides For Seven Brothers.

Joyce Like what?

Gordon Well, doesn't the title seem to suggest certain minimum casting requirements?

Joyce How do you mean?

Bernard There aren't enough of us, Joyce.

Joyce Oh. What about (*once again they all join in*) Oklahoma?

Gordon Same basic problem.

Joyce (*again with the others*) South Pacific?

Gordon No, Joyce!

Bernard We could have a crack at Robinson Crusoe.

Joyce You never want to do a musical.

Gordon It's not a matter of wanting, Joyce, it's a matter of what is possible.

Margaret Gordon's right, Joyce. Quite apart from the problem of numbers, you seem to have overlooked the fact that none of us can sing.

Joyce I can sing.

Gordon I'm sorry, Joyce, a musical's out of the question!

Joyce So we'll end up doing what you want, as always!

Gordon (*losing his temper*) Right! Okay! Fine! That's settled then. For the opening production of the season, Joyce will direct and star in our very own adaptation of that famous musical, Two Brides For Two Brothers!

Bernard Leave me out of this. I'm just the set-builder.

Gordon Sorry Joyce - make that Two Brides For One Brother.

Joyce We could recruit some new members. Put an ad in the Post Office.

Gordon Joyce, I'd rather be the recruitment officer for Sellafield than for us.

We've tried putting ads in the Post Office, and in the paper, and in the programmes - nobody wants to know. They've all seen us perform, for God's sake!

Joyce All right, all right. You've made your point.

Gordon Anybody else got any suggestions?

Margaret What about *(the others join in)* a nice little farce?

Gordon We always do a nice little farce.

Margaret It's what the people want.

Gordon What people? Our highly acclaimed production of Continental Quilt managed to sell seventeen tickets over three nights.

Bernard And three of those were Joyce's husband.

Joyce He had to give me a lift home.

Margaret They all enjoyed it, though.

Bernard Nobody laughed!

Margaret Just because there weren't any crude outbursts of laughter, it doesn't mean they didn't find it amusing. They were smiling internally.

Bernard Says who?

Margaret Joyce's husband, for one. And a friend of mine said it was the best thing we've done since "Oops, There Go My Trousers - More Tea, Vicar?".

Gordon It's the only thing we've done since "Oops, There Go My Trousers - More Tea, Vicar?" Let's face it. We're the laughing stock of the village.

Bernard The only thing they don't laugh at is our comedies.

Margaret I see. So what do you suggest - that we disband?

Joyce Oh, no! That would be a terrible shame.

Bernard This is the only chance I get to escape the wife all week.

Gordon No-one's suggesting that we disband, Margaret.

Margaret What then?

Gordon Well, luckily, your Chairman has a plan.

Margaret What plan?

Gordon A production that's going to knock 'em dead, and put bums on seats.

Margaret What production?

Gordon I have written a play.

Margaret You??

Gordon Don't sound so surprised, Margaret. I have written a play, and it's going to be our salvation.

Bernard Gordon, we've managed to knacker some of the best plays ever written. What makes you think yours is going to fair any better?

Gordon Sex.

Margaret I beg your pardon?

A Flying Ducks Publication

Gordon There's only thing that sells tickets these days - really sells tickets. Sex.

Margaret You're mad.

Bernard Shut up. Let him finish.

Margaret It's all right for you - you've just got to build the set.

Gordon Don't panic. Nobody's got to do anything embarrassing. We just make them think you do.

Margaret This all sounds very dodgy.

Gordon Not at all. The poster for my play will state a simple warning: ADULTS ONLY! THIS PLAY CONTAINS EXPLICIT SCENES OF NUDITY WHICH MAY SHOCK OR OFFEND. Then just watch them flock in.

Margaret And then what?

Gordon And then we give them a nice little farce.

Bernard Hold up a minute. You'll never get away with this. If we let them all come here thinking they're going to get a flash of Margaret's tits, we've got to deliver the goods.

Margaret You leave my tits out of this!

Bernard That's just my point - we can't. There'll be a riot.

Gordon No there won't. They'll all be far too embarrassed to admit that that's why they came. Nobody will say a word.

Margaret It's cheap and vulgar.

Gordon Yes.

Bernard It'll fill the place!

Gordon Yes.

Margaret What's it called, this play of yours?

Gordon Last Tango In Little Grimley.

Margaret Oh my God.

Joyce Is it a musical?

Gordon No Joyce, it's not a musical.

Joyce Oh.

Margaret I could never face the butcher again. He normally puts a poster up for me.

Bernard We won't need posters. We'll simply leak some information to Mrs Pimm.

Gordon Mrs Pimm. That's brilliant! The whole village will know in seconds.

Joyce What's it about?

Gordon Ah. That's the real masterstroke. It's about the butcher.

Margaret The butcher??

Gordon And the baker. And the candlestickmaker. And Mrs Pimm.

Margaret You're not making any sense, Gordon.

A Flying Ducks Publication

Gordon It's about Little Grimley. I've loosely based all the characters on people in the village.

Margaret How loosely?

Gordon Well, medium-loose. Loose-ish. Quite tight, actually.

Margaret Oh my God!

Bernard The sordid revelations of an apparently respectable village.

Margaret We'll be lynched.

Gordon No we won't! To lynch us, they're going to have to recognize themselves in the play, and they won't dare do that. Well, what do you think? Margaret?

Margaret It's madness.

Gordon Joyce?

Joyce Couldn't you put just one song in it?

Gordon Joyce, say yes and I'll write you a song.

Joyce Yes.

Gordon Bernard?

Bernard I still think Margaret ought to lob her tits out.

Margaret Margaret is not lobbing anything out, thank you very much.

Gordon What sort of set could you make for two hundred pounds?

Bernard Two hundred?

Gordon We could afford it on this one.

Bernard You can have bloody hydraulics for two hundred! And real brick walls!

Gordon Good man! Now you can see the potential! (*Turning to the impassive Margaret*) Margaret. I need your support.

Bernard So will she if she lobs those tits out.

Gordon Shut up, Bernard! Margaret?

Bernard Go on, Margaret. Give 'em an airing.

Margaret Will somebody drop a stage weight on that man's head?

Gordon Ignore him, Margaret. It's me who's asking you.

Margaret You realize that this will be the end of our society?

Gordon Well, we're almost dead anyway. What do you want to do? Go with a whimper, or an almighty bang?

Margaret Do I get the lead?

Gordon Of course.

Margaret And no flashing of tits?

Gordon No.

Margaret Unless of course I consider it absolutely essential to the plot.

Gordon As you wish.

Margaret I'll have to think it over.

Gordon I understand. If you say no, I'll offer the lead to Joyce.

A Flying Ducks Publication

Margaret I've thought it over. Let's do it.
Gordon Excellent. Any other business? Right, thank you, ladies and gentlemen. I suggest we re-convene at the same time next week to begin rehearsals.

Lights fade to black. Music. Lights up to reveal Gordon handing out scripts.

Gordon Sorry there wasn't time to get it typed up, but I'm sure we'll cope. There you go, Bernard.
Bernard I don't want one.
Gordon Yes you do, you're in it.
Bernard Hang on a minute! You're not getting me up on stage!
Gordon Why not?
Bernard Well, I can't act, for a start!
Gordon You don't have to act, Bernard. Just do what the rest of us do.
Bernard No way.
Gordon Bernard, you've got to! I need four actors. Everybody else is playing three parts - you're just doing the butcher. Look, if you don't do it, the whole thing's off.
Joyce Come on, Bernard, you've done it before.
Bernard It's a bit bloody different playing the back end of a horse in a kid's panto - I mean, look - this is a speaking part.
Gordon Look, Bernard, I'm going to be brutally honest with you. If I'd got a choice between you and Dustin Hoffman, you probably wouldn't get the part. But I haven't. So you're doing it. End of argument. Right, let's go. The first page is just my notes. So, take it from the top of page two, Margaret's entrance. Ready, Bernard?
Bernard I'm not in yet.
Gordon Yes you are. Top of page two.
Bernard Where?
Gordon Top of page two. (*No response from Bernard*) Top of page two. (*Bernard continues to study the script in silent panic*) Butcher. (*Getting tenser*) Top of page two. Not the bottom. Not the middle. (*Finally exploding*) Look, I know you're not an actor, Bernard, but I was hoping you could read!
Bernard (*waving his script at Gordon*) Look! Top of page two! No bloody butcher!
Gordon That's page three!
Bernard It's my page two!
Gordon What happened to page two?
Joyce I've got two page two's.

A Flying Ducks Publication

Gordon Aha!
Joyce But no page three.
Gordon Bernard, have you got two page three's?
Bernard No.
Margaret I've got two page three's.
Gordon Right.
Margaret But no page four.
Bernard I might be able to help you out there. I've got three of the buggers.
Gordon Joyce, you give Bernard your other page three...
Bernard I've already got a page three.
Gordon So what's the problem?
Bernard No bloody page two!
Gordon Who had two page two's?
Joyce Me.
Gordon Right, give your page two to Bernard.
Joyce Both of them?
Gordon No! Just one! Now, Margaret, give your other page three to Joyce. Bernard - give one of your page fours to Margaret. Everybody happy now?
Bernard I've still got too many page fours.
Gordon (*taking the page, and screwing it up*) Right. Let's go. Top of page two - Margaret's entrance. (*The phone rings*) Oh bloody hell! Start reading it through.

Exit Gordon.

Margaret Right, my entrance. Ready, Bernard?
Bernard I suppose so.
Margaret Right, er...Margaret enters...what am I carrying?
Bernard What?
Margaret It says Margaret enters carrying a something, I can't read his writing.
Bernard Er...carrying...a limp.
Margaret Oh, right. Which leg?
Bernard Why?
Margaret It's important to get the details of the character right, Bernard, you'll find this out.
Bernard It's just a read-through, it doesn't matter which leg.
Margaret The left, then.
Bernard If you like.
Margaret Or do you prefer the right?

A Flying Ducks Publication

Bernard No, I prefer the left, just get on with it.

Margaret (*limping in dramatically*) "Morning, Gerald!"

Bernard (*incredibly woodenly*) "Morning, Mrs Duffield. What can I get you today?"

Margaret "I fancy a bit of rump."

Bernard (*without expression*) "Don't we all, Mrs Duffield, don't we all."

Margaret "Can I"...this is appalling...

Joyce Come on, don't break the flow.

Margaret "Can I have a look at your loins?"

Bernard "Anytime, Mrs Duffield. Just don't let your husband find out."

Margaret It's not exactly Chekhov, is it.

Joyce I think it's quite good! Carry on.

Margaret "You know, Gerald, my husband just doesn't realize how much meat has gone up."

Bernard "No, I bet he doesn't."

Margaret "Oh, you are saucy, Gerald." I'm sorry, I can't do this. No-one, but no-one, is going to buy tickets to see this garbage, and when Gordon comes back, I'm going to tell him so.

Enter Gordon.

Gordon There we go! Our first ticket sales. Fifteen seats for Saturday.

Joyce Fifteen! That's more than we've ever had in on one night!

Gordon I told you, Joyce, sex sells tickets.

Bernard Who was it?

Gordon The Lively Ladies Over Fifties Club.

Margaret You are joking?

Gordon No. Looks like Mrs Pimm is doing her job very effectively.

Margaret Do they know it's a sex comedy?

Gordon I think they're relying on the fact.

Margaret The dirty old sods!

Gordon More a case of nostalgia with them. Still, every ticket counts. Right, how are you getting on with the opening scene?

Joyce Well, Margaret thinks...

Margaret Actually, Gordon, I think we've cracked it. How's this? "Morning, Gerald!"

Bernard "Morning, Mrs Duffield."

Gordon Hold it...

Bernard "What can I get you today?"

A Flying Ducks Publication

Gordon Hold it, hold it. Bernard, come on. You're a butcher. Be butcher! Butchers are loud, rosy-cheeked, vivacious.
Bernard Ours isn't. Ours is a surly old bugger.
Gordon Well, I think we can allow ourselves a bit of artistic licence.
Margaret Bernard's artistic licence expired years ago.
Bernard (*marching off*) Right, stuff your script!
Gordon Bernard! Bernard, Bernard. Come back! Margaret didn't mean it - did you, Margaret?
Margaret If he wants to be an actor he's got to learn to take a little criticism.
Bernard I don't want to be an actor - remember? I'm a set-builder.
Margaret It's a pity your sets aren't as wooden as your performances.
Bernard Bollocks!
Gordon Bernard!!!

Bernard storms out, and is eventually dragged back by Gordon.

Gordon Well, it's nice to see the old team spirit is back with a vengeance. Now look, I'm the director, here. I'll hand out the criticism when it's due, and it will good, sound, constructive criticism, and we'll all take it in good heart, okay? Good. Right, now, Bernard, that was shite. Do it again. And this time put some life into it.
Bernard (*the same wooden delivery as previously, but just a little louder*) "Morning, Mrs Duffield."
Gordon Better...
Bernard "What can I get you today?"
Gordon Much better!
Margaret (*dragging her left leg heavily*) "I fancy a bit of rump."
Gordon Hold it. Margaret...
Margaret (*touchily*) You don't like the way I'm doing it, do you?
Gordon No, no...
Margaret It's not an easy line to deliver, you know.
Gordon Margaret, Margaret! You're doing it fine. I just wondered what you'd done to your leg.
Margaret My leg?
Gordon Are you in pain?
Margaret I'm acting, Gordon. Just obeying stage directions. Margaret enters carrying a limp.
Gordon A lamp. Margaret enters carrying a lamp.
Margaret It's your bloody awful handwriting!

Gordon Look, I'm sorry, I haven't exactly had time to get the thing published.
Margaret So I'm carrying a lamp, not a limp.
Gordon Precisely.
Margaret All right, just as long as I know. These little details are important, you know.
Gordon Right, can we get on?
Margaret (*she pauses, and settles herself to deliver the line*) Which hand do you want the lamp in?
Gordon Look, skip this scene. I'm getting bored with it. Move on to page four. Joyce, you're on.
Joyce Who am I playing?
Gordon You, Joyce, are playing you, Joyce.
Joyce Who?
Gordon You're playing yourself, Joyce.
Joyce (*doubtful*) Playing myself?
Gordon Yes.
Joyce Me?
Gordon Well, I thought you were the obvious one for the part.
Joyce Oh. I'm not sure I can play myself, Gordon.
Gordon You're the right height. You've got the accent off to a tee - what's the problem here? Just be yourself.
Joyce And do what?
Gordon Ah! It came to me in a flash of inspiration. You want to do a song, right?
Joyce Yes.
Gordon But this isn't a musical, it's a farce.
Bernard You can say that again.
Gordon So I thought, how can I get a song into a farce? Then, it hit me.
Joyce What?
Gordon You're playing you, practising for the forthcoming production of Seven Brides For Seven Brothers - so you get to do a song from the show!
Joyce We're doing Seven Brides For Seven Brothers after all?
Gordon No, Joyce, watch my lips. My play, is a play about an Amateur Dramatic Society, with you in it, performing a musical.
Joyce Us, you mean?
Gordon Yes, us, if you like, but it could be someone else.
Joyce Are we doing the musical or not?
Gordon No!! We're pretending to do it! It's a play! You're in a play, about a play. (*Joyce stares at him blankly*) Never mind. Just read the words on the

script. Page four.

Joyce Where do I stand?

Gordon You don't stand. You lie down. You're in the bath.

Joyce The bath?

Gordon What better place to rehearse the song?

Joyce With no clothes on?

Gordon We'll cover you with bubbles.

Joyce I'm not taking my clothes off, Gordon.

Gordon You can wear a bikini. You'll be covered in bubbles.

Joyce I'm not wearing a bikini, Gordon.

Gordon (*exploding*) All right, fine! You can wear a bloody duffle coat for all I care. I don't give a damn. Just don't pull the hood up! Right, you're in the bath, singing away, one of the big rousing numbers from Seven Brides, and I come bursting in, and...

Joyce Who are you?

Gordon I'm the vicar.

Joyce What's the vicar doing in my bathroom?

Gordon He hears you singing, and thinks you're calling for help.

Joyce What's he doing in my house?

Gordon Look, I'm not going to stand here and explain the whole plot. You'll have to pick it up as we go along.

Margaret It's a bit tricky when you keep skipping pages.

Gordon You were taking too long.

Margaret We'd have been halfway through by now if you'd let me carry on.

The phone rings.

Bernard I'll get it.

Exit Bernard.

Gordon All right, all right. Let's just crack on. Joyce, start singing.

Joyce What?

Gordon Anything. You're in the bath - sing! (*She does*) Good. Right, now I come bursting in and say...(*he checks his script*)...oh, shit!

Margaret Isn't that a bit strong for a vicar?

Gordon I haven't got a page four. (*Margaret rescues the crumpled page four from the floor, and hands it to him*) Thank you. Right, I burst in and say "Are you all right? Oops! Mrs Pilkington, I'm so sorry, I never, I...I..., well I never!"

A Flying Ducks Publication

(Joyce, oblivious, is still singing) Joyce...Joyce! Shut up! Script!

Joyce Oh, right. *(Pause)* Now?

Gordon Yes, now, Joyce, before one of us dies.

Joyce "Oh! Vicar. It's you."

Gordon "Yes. I could have sworn I heard a cry for help."

Joyce "I was just rehearsing for the forthcoming show."

Gordon "I'm terribly sorry, I...I, well, I think I'd better leave."

Joyce "Yes, I think that would be best."

Gordon "Right, then, I'll leave, then.

Joyce "Right."

Margaret Is this in iambic pentameter?

Gordon Shut up. You're on.

Margaret I am?

Gordon Mrs Stodgeworthy.

Margaret Oh, right. "Mrs Pilkington, are you all...arrgh! Vicar!"

Gordon "Why, Mrs Stodgeworthy! I...I...well I was just...

Margaret "I can see what you were doing, vicar!"

Gordon "No, no, you've got it all wrong, I just came to have a look....I mean...I just came to lend a hand...I mean, she was just rehearsing..."

Margaret "Spare me the sordid details!"

Gordon Great. Then you storm out - well, go on, storm, storm - and return a few seconds later to say...

Margaret "The bishop will hear of this!"

Gordon Terrific! Well, what do you think, Bernard?

Bernard *(entering)* I think it's the biggest load of crap I've ever seen in my life.

Gordon *(hurt)* Thank you.

Bernard But it's just sold another thirty-five tickets for Saturday night.

Joyce Thirty-five?!

Bernard A block-booking from the Young Farmer's Club. I think we're in business!

Lights fade, music. Lights up to reveal Margaret and Joyce, with scripts, rehearsing a scene sotto voce. They are wearing token Oxfam hats and coats to denote a dress rehearsal. Bernard, wearing his butcher's apron and cap, is sitting reading the local newspaper. Gordon, in a black top and dog-collar, is wandering around with the telephone on a long lead.

Gordon I'm sorry, Friday and Saturday are both sold out - we've still got a few tickets for the Thursday night....you can? Okay, I'll reserve those for you - two on the door for Thursday night, that's fine....no problem. Thank you, vicar. (*Replacing the receiver*) Right - where were we?

Margaret Top of page forty-six.

Gordon Yes, what I was getting at, Joyce - you know that way when people get angry, how they tend to talk louder and worry less about their diction and move their arms about and stuff like that - well, I'll like you to try and imitate that sort of thing. You know, it's called acting.

Joyce I'm doing my best!

Gordon I know, I know. Perhaps you could do it better without the scripts.

Margaret Now, steady on!

Gordon Come on, Margaret. We open tomorrow night. It's about time we tried it.

Bernard Hey, read this.

Gordon Not now, Bernard. I'm rehearsing.

Bernard You'll want to read this.

Gordon Later.

Bernard Read it! (*He thrusts his newspaper under Gordon's eyes, which gradually widen as he reads the article Bernard has found*).

Margaret What is it?

Gordon Read. (*He hands the newspaper to Margaret. Joyce gathers in to read too*).

Margaret He can't do this!

Gordon Looks like he's done it.

Joyce A cabaret club!?

Bernard You can't really blame him. We haven't exactly raked the money in for him, have we?

Joyce He could at least have told us.

Margaret Does he honestly think that people are going to prefer this garbage to good live theatre.

Gordon No, but he obviously thinks they'll prefer it to us.

Margaret Opens April 24th. So, this really is the Last Tango In Little Grimley.

Joyce What are we going to do?

Gordon (*determined*) I'll tell you what we're going to do, Joyce. We're going to give them a night they'll never forget. Come on! Let's show 'em what we're made of. Positions everybody. Let's do it without scripts!

Bernard exits.

Margaret Will you prompt?

Gordon All right. Top of forty-six. Margaret's line..."I'd like to have a word with you, Mrs Pilkington..."

Margaret "I'd like to have a word with you, Mrs Pilkington." (*There's a pause, then she starts clicking her fingers in frustration for the prompt*) Sorry.

Gordon "What's going on..."

Margaret "What's going on?"

Gordon ..."between"...

Margaret "Between. Between...my husband and you?".

Gordon "You and my husband".

Margaret Same thing. "What's going on between you and my husband?"

Joyce (*pause*) Is it me now?

Gordon Yes Joyce, it's you now.

Joyce Er...how dare you?

Gordon Yes.

Joyce (*very tamely*) "How dare you."

Gordon Anger, Joyce, anger!! Look, like me, now. I'm angry, I'm shouting! I'm moving my arms about! Now, come on, Joyce. Frighten me!

Joyce (*Just as tamely, but this time flapping her arms like a flightless bird*) "How dare you." Did that frighten you, Gordon?

Gordon (*head in hands*) It certainly did, Joyce. It scared the shit out of me. Look! We've got one day left. One! Then the biggest audience you've ever seen in your life is going to descend on this place. No-one even knows their lines! Now, come on! Again, same place!

The two actresses start to go over the same few lines again, but Bernard enters carrying a stage flat, drops it in front of them, and starts hammering loudly.

Gordon Hold it! Bernard...Bernard!!! (*He stops hammering*) What the hell do you think you're doing?

Bernard What's it look like?

Gordon It looks like you're trying to ruin my rehearsal.

Bernard I'm trying to build the bloody set!

Gordon Well you can't do it now!

Bernard When would you like me to do it? Tomorrow night? Do you want me to wait till the bloody audience gets here? Perhaps I could ask some of them to give me a hand.

Gordon Can't you wait till we have a tea break?

Bernard What am I supposed to do till then? When do I get a bloody tea-break?

Gordon Look, calm down. Just let me get to the end, and we'll all give you a hand, I promise.

A Flying Ducks Publication

Bernard I don't need your help.
Gordon Well, I was just offering.
Margaret Nice to see the old team spirit is back with a vengeance.
Bernard I don't want to be here till midnight, you know.
Gordon Just find something else to do, just for five minutes - that's all. Then it's all yours.
Bernard Five minutes.

He exits, cursing under his breath.

Gordon All right, once more. This had better be the last time.
Margaret "I'd like a word with you, Mrs Pilkington. What's going on between my husband and you?"
Joyce *(flapping her arms)* "How dare you."
Gordon Joyce...
Margaret "I'll tell you how I dare..."

Gordon Hold it. Joyce. *(Imitating the flapping)* What's this?
Joyce You're the one that told me to move my arms, Gordon. You said it would make me look angry.
Gordon Yes. But an angry person, Joyce. An angry person. Not an angry ostrich. *(Despairingly)* Try it again.

They once again start the scene and, after a few seconds, the lights start flashing wildly, then go out. We hear Gordon's frustrated cry from the darkness.

Gordon Bernard!!!
Bernard What's the matter now?
Gordon Stop pratting about with the lights! I'm trying to rehearse!
Bernard I'm trying to set the buggers! Stages don't light themselves up you know.
Gordon Can't you do it later?
Bernard I'm building the set later - remember?
Gordon We can't see the scripts!
Bernard What do you want to see the scripts for? You're supposed to know the words by now.
Gordon All right, Bernard. You win. Put the lights on. Come and build the damn set.

The lights come on.

A Flying Ducks Publication

Margaret What about the rehearsal?

Gordon Stuff the rehearsal! We'll have to go on as we are. What the hell does it matter anyway? We're finished! I'm off to the pub.

Gordon storms out. Margaret gives him a haughty stare before turning to Joyce.

Margaret Prima donna.

Lights fade to black, music. Lights up to reveal the four protagonists seated as before.

Gordon Right, Joyce, treasurer's report.

Joyce Well, in total, we spent two hundred and seventy-two pounds and fifty new pence on materials, props, costumes and set. Total money taken for ticket sales was....eight hundred and forty-nine pounds!

Margaret Wow!

Gordon That means we can pay off our debts, and have some to spare. I suggest we donate what's left over to a local charity.

Joyce I'll arrange a cheque, Gordon.

Margaret Well, I've got to hand it to you, Gordon. As far as Little Grimley is concerned, you're the most successful playwright this century.

Gordon I think the one we've really got to thank is you, Margaret.

Joyce Hear, hear!

They give her a small round of applause.

Gordon That was a stroke of genius, Margaret.

Joyce And so unexpected.

Margaret Let's face it, they were on the verge of booing us off. It was do or die.

Gordon Nevertheless, it was a major personal sacrifice.

Margaret You should see the letters I've had. Seventeen offers of marriage - three of which I intend to follow up. And one offer of something quite disgusting, which I also intend to follow up.

Gordon Well, unless anyone has any other business? No? In that case I declare the meeting closed, and move that we officially disband Little Grimley Amateur Dramatic Society.

There's a moment's sad silence.

A Flying Ducks Publication

Bernard Well, that's it then, I suppose. I'm going to miss the old place.

Joyce Twelve years we've been here.

Margaret A cabaret club. I suppose it had to happen eventually.

Bernard At least we went out with a bang.

Joyce And a song.

Margaret And a capacity crowd.

Bernard First time ever in living memory. Or should I say "mammary?"

Margaret Thank you, Bernard. I'll miss your subtle sense of humour. I always did.

Bernard Well, I'll be toddling off, then. Pity we didn't get a glimpse of the left one, Margaret. I've heard it's even better.

Gordon (*suddenly producing a script*) Well, maybe this is your chance, Bernard.

Margaret What's that?

Gordon The sequel. More Tangos in Little Grimley. We already have massive advanced ticket sales. The only problem is Mrs Pimm has asked for 5% commission.

Margaret I don't understand. What about the cabaret club?

Gordon Ah. I had a call from Stan Fellows. Apparently we're just the sort of act he's looking for. We're booked for the opening Saturday night. Strictly professional, of course. (*They all stare at him, dumbfounded*). Well? What are we waiting for? Let's start rehearsing. Margaret, I think you need to work on that wiggle...

Music covers their excited babble, as lights fade. Curtain.

A Flying Ducks Publication

Joining The Club

Jenny enters, carrying a package from the Chemists. She takes off her jacket and, with apparent trepidation, opens the package, which contains a home-pregnancy test. Looking tense and worried, she skims through the instructions, and then exits with the test strip. After a few moments, the toilet flushes, and she re-enters, wearing a rubber glove, tentatively holding the test strip. She goes back to the instructions, checks her watch, and then leaves the test strip on a coffee table.

She paces nervously, and on more than one occasion goes to look at the strip, but checks herself after consulting her watch. Finally, convinced she has waited the requisite amount of time, she grabs the test strip, plucks up courage, and thrusts it in front of her eyes. She immediately looks away, takes a deep breath, and has a second, more considered look. Tears well up in her eyes - though the audience is left wondering whether they are tears of excitement or disappointment.

We hear the front door open, and Jenny is snapped out of her emotional state, into one of instant panic. She hastily looks around for somewhere to hide the test strip. There's a loaded tea-tray on the table, and she irrationally drops the test strip into the teapot, and covers it with the cosy.

At the last moment, she spots the pregnancy testing kit box on the armchair. She leaps into the chair, thrusting the box behind a cushion, and buries her head behind a woman's magazine. Enter Tom, her husband, looking tense and depressed. He slams the door, slams down his keys and briefcase, and makes straight for the drinks cabinet, where he pours himself a large whiskey, before finally slumping into the armchair. Jenny pops her head around the magazine, and forces an innocent greeting.

Jenny Had a good day?

Tom It depends how you look at it.

Jenny Had a row with Alex again?

Tom Alex? Alex? Let me see...yes, he was on the list.

A Flying Ducks Publication

Jenny That bad, eh?

Tom He brought in his baby snaps today.

Jenny Oh, God. I meant to send them a card. How's the baby?

Tom That depends who you talk to. Derek reckons he's fabulous, cute, and just like his father. I reckon he's obnoxious, malformed, and just like his father.

Jenny Don't be horrible.

Tom Who's being horrible? He's the one performing the dodgy genetic experiments. God knows what sort of weird mutant he's created this time.

Jenny You're vile.

Tom You shouldn't use words like vile so liberally. You'll have nothing left to describe this baby when you see it.

Jenny And that's what's put you in such a bad mood, is it? Alex's little baby.

There's an awkward pause. Tom sits sulkily behind a newspaper. Jenny plucks up courage to reveal her secret.

Jenny Tom...

Tom Derek announced the promotion today.

Jenny And? (*Tom smiles, cryptically*) You didn't...

Tom That's right.

Jenny (*excitedly*) Oh, Tom!

Tom I didn't.

Jenny Stop pratting about, Tom - did you get it or not?

Tom Not.

Jenny Oh, no. I'm really sorry.

Tom Yeah.

Jenny Who?

Tom Alex.

Jenny Alex? But you're a far better salesman than he is!

Tom I know.

Jenny You told me he'd failed miserably with his targets.

Tom He has.

Jenny Then why him?

Tom You've just answered it yourself. A sales manager doesn't sell - he manages. By promoting Alex they don't lose valuable business.

Jenny But that's crazy! You're being penalised for being successful!

Tom Welcome to the world of selling. Alex gets a new car and a salary increase. I get bigger targets for next year.

Jenny Have you made your feelings known to Derek?

A Flying Ducks Publication

Tom You could say that, yes.

Jenny And?

Tom Oh, he threw out the usual platitudes, you know, the usual carrots. Hinting at other opportunities round the corner.

Jenny Perhaps you'd better stop working so hard. That's obviously the secret to success. (*She makes another attempt to reveal her secret*) Tom...

Tom There is another reason I didn't get the job.

Jenny What reason?

Tom Oh, I'm not a member of the club.

Jenny What club?

Tom The baby club.

Jenny Oh don't be stupid.

Tom I'm not being stupid, Jenny! I've watched it happening. (*Beginning quietly, and working into a frenzy*) "Hello, Alex? How's little Elliot?" "Oh. he's a cracker - smiled yesterday, you know!" "Oh, you just wait till the teeth start coming in! Amy's got three now! Getting any sleep?" "Now and again - you know how it is!" "Tell you what, why don't you and Mary come round for dinner one night - bring little Elliot - see what Amy makes of him!" "Thanks Derek, I'd like that - I'd like that a lot!" "Oh, by the way, here's that twelve litre tub of nappy-rash cream I promised you!"

Jenny You don't like young children, do you?

Tom Oh, young children are all right. It's young parents I can't stand. You can spot them a mile away - bloodshot eyes, sickly, vacant grin. Like a bunch of born-again Christians, patronising everybody who hasn't procreated in the last five minutes.

Jenny Tom, I've got something to tell you.

Tom (*getting up*) And I've got something to tell you.

Jenny This is important.

Tom So is this.

Jenny Oh. Right. Okay, you first.

Tom I've resigned.

Jenny You've done what?

Tom Resigned.

Jenny I don't understand.

Tom Don't you? (*Tossing her a dictionary*) Here, look it up. It begins with R.

Jenny So does rash!

Tom There's nothing rash about it. I've been thinking about it for a while. This promotion thing was just the last straw.

Jenny But...but you can't just give up your job.

Tom Why not? It's a boring job. I'm bored. In fact, it's the most boring job in the world. It's turning me into the most boring person in the world.

Jenny Don't be ridiculous.

Tom I'm not being ridiculous.

Jenny What about Alex?

Tom Okay, the second most boring person in the world.

Jenny And that woman who used to collect our jumble...

Tom Look, let's not quibble about details! I'm in the top six - all right? That's enough.

Jenny You're over-reacting.

Tom No, I'm just doing what I should have done years ago.

Jenny Going on the dole.

Tom Not necessarily.

Jenny What then?

Tom Maybe I'll start my own business.

Jenny Doing what?

Tom I don't know yet.

Jenny Oh, so you've got it all thought out.

Tom Look! Get off my back will you? Have you got any idea what it's like to spend eight, nine, ten hours a day in a place you hate? No, of course you haven't! (*Clutching at Jenny's magazine*) You love your job. It's exciting. It's interesting. You also happen to be one of the best paid editors in London. You earn more in one week than I do in a month.

Jenny You're exaggerating.

Tom Am I?

Jenny I suppose it takes me about a week and a half to earn what you earn in a month.

Tom Really? Oh, goody! Now I feel a lot better about myself.

Jenny So all of a sudden you resent that fact that I have a good job!

Tom Resent it? Good God, no! I'm jealous of it! And it's not all of a sudden. I've been jealous of it for years. Don't you understand? I want to do something interesting as well. I want to be successful.

Jenny (*more sympathetically*) Look, I'm sorry about the promotion. I really am. And I'm sorry the job's a bit boring at the moment.

Tom It's not a bit boring at the moment, Jenny. It's a lot boring - all the time.

Jenny All right! So it's a lot boring all the time...at the moment. But you can't just give up everything in a...in a fit of passion.

Tom You keep saying that. You can't. You can't. Why not?

Jenny Why not? Because!

A Flying Ducks Publication

Tom Because what? Money? You know damn well we don't need my money. We can live comfortably off what you earn for as long as we like.

Jenny What about self-esteem?

Tom Self what?

Jenny Esteem.

Tom Oh! You mean that special kick I get every time I win a repeat order for a tractor part?

Jenny So what are you going to do? Stay at home all day and rot?

Tom Well why not!

Jenny You'd soon get b...(*she stops herself*)

Tom What?

Jenny Nothing.

Tom Bored? Is that what you were going to say? I'll get bored?

Jenny No.

Tom What then?

Jenny I wasn't going to say bored.

Tom What then? Come on.

Jenny Fed up.

Tom Oh, fed up! Not bored. Fed up.

Jenny Look, you can't give up your job, okay, not now. You just can't.

Tom Just give me one good reason why not.

Jenny Because I'm pregnant!

Tom (*after a long pause*) What's that supposed to mean?

Jenny (*tossing back the dictionary*) Here! Look it up. It begins with C for copulation.

Tom Is this a joke?

Jenny Does it sound like a joke?

Tom No.

Jenny It isn't a joke.

Tom You said you were pregnant.

Jenny Yes.

Tom But...how?

Jenny It's called sex, Tom. Do you remember it? Those three little stars on the year planner.

Tom But we don't have sex! I mean, not proper sex...I mean, not without...taking precautions.

Jenny Well obviously the precautions didn't work.

Tom Your birthday. It was your bloody birthday! You were drunk.

Jenny I'd got a feeling this was going to be my fault.

A Flying Ducks Publication

Tom I knew it wasn't on right! It was all bloody twisted.
Jenny You're the one that's all twisted.
Tom You opened the packet with your teeth. I bet you bit right through it!
Jenny Don't you dare try and blame this on me! Three years I was on the pill. Three years of shoving drugs down my throat every single day just so you didn't have to think twice. Well, not this time, pal. Joint responsibility.
Tom Pregnant! Jesus Christ! What are we going to do?
Jenny I'll tell you what we're going to do, Tom. We're going to have a baby.
Tom Is it mine?

She slaps his face hard.

Tom Was that a yes?
Jenny Balls!
Tom I accept your apology.
Jenny You'll accept my bloody knee in your groin in a minute.
Tom All right, all right. Let's calm down. Pregnant. That means...you're going to have a baby.
Jenny We're going to have a baby.
Tom Right. Okay. Pregnant. That means...a baby.
Jenny Normally, yes.
Tom How do you know?
Jenny I learnt about it at school.
Tom I mean, how do you know you're pregnant?
Jenny Oh. (*She produces the kit from behind the cushion*) I bought this. (*She hands Tom the box. He pulls out a test strip, and stares at it blankly*) You have to urinate on it.
Tom I do?
Jenny No, me you fool! If you're pregnant, two blue bands appear. Look.

She retrieves her test strip from the teapot as Tom continues to examine the kit with morbid curiosity.

Tom But these are brown.
Jenny That's because they've been in the teapot.
Tom Of course. How silly of me.
Jenny I'll have to go to the doctor. But it's almost certain.
Tom Your job - what about your job?
Jenny I'll stay on until Christmas.

A Flying Ducks Publication

Tom And then you'll have a baby.
Jenny No, then we'll have a baby.
Tom All right. Let's think about this. We can cope with this.
Jenny I'm glad to hear it.
Tom Christmas. That's what...six months? We can save a lot of money in six months. Enough to tide us over until you're ready to go back.
Jenny Back where?
Tom To work.
Jenny I'm not going back to work, Tom. I'm leaving at Christmas.
Tom It's all right, I know about this. Alex has told me about it - they have to keep your job open for you - it's the law.
Jenny Tom, you're not hearing me. I don't want my job back.
Tom But you love your job!
Jenny I like my job. I'll love my baby. I want to leave work and look after my baby.
Tom But you can't!
Jenny Why not?
Tom Oh, I see. I've got it. I can't leave work. I can't change my lifestyle. But you can.
Jenny I'm the one having the baby!
Tom No, we're the ones having the baby, remember?
Jenny Oh, Tom! You're impossible!
Tom I just...I just can't believe you could go ahead and do something as important as this without at least consulting me.
Jenny Consulting you? Consulting you? Tom, you were right there on top of me!
Tom Underneath.
Jenny All right! Underneath! Either way, you were right in there when the decision was being made.
Tom You know what I mean.
Jenny No, I don't know what you mean! This was an accident, Tom. You know? Fifty-fifty. We both lose our no claims bonus. And if you want to talk about consultation, what about consulting me before you resign your job?
Tom That's hardly in the same league.
Jenny The principle is the same.
Tom The money is not the same.
Jenny The money is irrelevant.
Tom No, no. The money is very relevant. The money is vital. Do you know how much it costs to run a baby these days?
Jenny It's not a car, Tom. You don't run babies. And it just so happens I do

know. We did an article on it last month.

Tom And?

Jenny And...okay, it costs about three thousand pounds a year to have a baby.

Tom No, it costs about forty-three thousand pounds a year to have a baby, remember? Because before you can kiss the baby, you have to kiss goodbye to one of the best-paid female jobs in the country.

Jenny Well, I'm very sorry. What would you like me to do? Give birth at my desk? Put the baby in the out-tray? I know, I could give it to my secretary to sort out - "Here, file this under B!"

Tom You could go back to work after a few months!

Jenny And do what? Dump the baby with a child-minder?

Tom Why not?

Jenny Because I'm not going to be a week-end mother, Tom! I want our baby to know where its home is!

Tom And where's that, eh? Where's its home going to be? Because it's certainly not going to be here.

Jenny Don't be ridiculous.

Tom Oh, you find that ridiculous, do you? In that case, tell me, please. How are we supposed to pay the mortgage?

Jenny I don't know yet.

Tom Oh, you don't know yet!

Jenny (*bawling*) I haven't got all the answers, Tom! All I know is I'm going to have a baby! Your baby! Jesus Christ - this is supposed to be a happy occasion. You're supposed to be happy!

Tom (*screaming angrily*) I am happy!! (*Quieter*) I'm bloody delirious.

The row has reached its climax. Tom's temper blows itself out, and Jenny is in tears.

Tom I'm sorry. It's just...such a shock.

Jenny (*recovering*) Look, we'll work something out...about the money. Tom, this is more important than money. This is us. This is our baby.

Tom I just...I just don't think we can afford this mortgage on my salary.

Jenny You haven't got a salary - you've resigned.

Tom Oh, God! I'd forgotten that.

Jenny Look, I know it's not the ideal solution, but, just for now, to tide us over, couldn't you withdraw your resignation?

Tom I don't think so.

Jenny Look, we can start looking for another job for you straight away - but without the pressure. It's always much better if you're employed.